AFFIRMATIONS

for TEENAGE BOYS

GW00482078

Name:________________________________

First Edition: 2020

FIRST THINGS FIRST.....

What are affirmations? Affirmations are positive statements that you repeat to yourself daily to help you reprogram your subconscious mind to get past negative , self-sabotaging beliefs and thoughts. They help change the way that you think and feel about yourself and your life, and help you focus on positive goals.

THEY ARE ABOUT YOU!

How to use this book: In order to personalize and use affirmations effectively, you need to first figure out which negative thoughts or behaviors you want to change. You'll begin with a bit of self-analysis, then look at suggestions for affirmations about various parts of your life, see which ones resonate with you, and then write a list of your own affirmations. If some make you feel truly uncomfortable, it may be a sign that they are exactly the ones you most need to repeat!

There will be an Affirmation Tracker to help you remember to say your affirmations daily, and space to journal your feelings and how they are changing.

REASONS I ROCK

DREAMS

WHO AM I?

MY SUPPORT

- ____________
- ____________
- ____________
- ____________
- ____________
- ____________
- ____________
- ____________

NEGATIVE BEHAVIORS I WANT TO CHANGE

NEGATIVE THOUGHTS I WANT TO CHANGE

AFFIRMATIONS: YOUNG MEN

1. I am a leader, not a follower.
2. I am in touch with my feelings.
3. I don't have to conform to other's expectations.
4. It's okay to just be me.
5. I am worthwhile.
6. I have a lot to offer.
7. I don't have to be perfect.
8. I stand up for myself.
9. I am a team player.
10. I am a spiritual being.
11. ______________________________
12. ______________________________
13. ______________________________
14. ______________________________
15. ______________________________
16. ______________________________
17. ______________________________
18. ______________________________
19. ______________________________
20. ______________________________

HOW I FEEL ABOUT BEING A GUY

AFFIRMATIONS: PEER PRESSURE

1. I don't have to be like everyone else to be valued.
2. I am a leader. I don't follow the crowd.
3. I get to decide what is right for me.
4. I have the right to say "no" and mean it.
5. Popularity does not predict success.
6. What others think of me is their business, not mine.
7. I know right from wrong.
8. I choose to be around people who love and respect me.
9. The choices I make now will determine who I become.
10. I stand up to bullies.
11. ______________________________
12. ______________________________
13. ______________________________
14. ______________________________
15. ______________________________
16. ______________________________
17. ______________________________
18. ______________________________
19. ______________________________
20. ______________________________

HOW I FEEL ABOUT PEER PRESSURE

AFFIRMATIONS: BODY IMAGE

1. I love my body.
2. I am my own perfect self.
3. My body is a fine-tuned machine.
4. I am comfortable in my own skin.
5. I am good looking and attractive, both inside and out.
6. I eat well, exercise and get plenty of rest.
7. I am at my perfect, healthy size.
8. I enjoy exercise and the way it makes me feel.
9. I embrace the body that God has given me.
10. I am healthy and strong -- I take good care of myself.
11. ______________________________
12. ______________________________
13. ______________________________
14. ______________________________
15. ______________________________
16. ______________________________
17. ______________________________
18. ______________________________
19. ______________________________
20. ______________________________

HOW I FEEL ABOUT MY BODY

AFFIRMATIONS: FRIENDSHIP

1. I have good friends who love and respect me for myself.
2. I treat others with patience, compassion & understanding.
3. I am a good friend.
4. I treat others with respect & value them for themselves.
5. I treat myself and others with forgiveness.
6. I am a good listener. I listen with my head & with my heart.
7. I give love, joy and laughter to others.
8. I terminate toxic friendships.
9. I am supportive and encourage others.
10. I value friends who encourage me to do the right thing.
11. ______________________________
12. ______________________________
13. ______________________________
14. ______________________________
15. ______________________________
16. ______________________________
17. ______________________________
18. ______________________________
19. ______________________________
20. ______________________________

HOW I FEEL ABOUT MY FRIENDS

AFFIRMATIONS: SCHOOL

1. I am moving towards my future.
2. I am curious.
3. I am grateful to have the opportunity to learn.
4. I am enthusiastic about my studies.
5. I see value in a well-rounded education.
6. I am committed to learning new things.
7. I respect and like my teachers.
8. I have the intelligence and intuition to do well in school.
9. I am mastering social skills & learning to deal with others.
10. I have a strong work ethic and complete my assignments.
11. ______________________________
12. ______________________________
13. ______________________________
14. ______________________________
15. ______________________________
16. ______________________________
17. ______________________________
18. ______________________________
19. ______________________________
20. ______________________________

HOW I FEEL ABOUT SCHOOL

AFFIRMATIONS: SELF-ESTEEM

1. I have a lot to offer the world.
2. I love the person I am and the person I am becoming.
3. I am confident in myself and trust myself completely.
4. I am worthy of respect from myself and from others.
5. I love and accept myself unconditionally for who I am.
6. I am true to myself.
7. I am deserving of love.
8. Nobody can make me feel inferior.
9. I embrace my own inner worth and strength.
10. I do not need to rely on others to be happy & fulfilled.
11. ______________________________
12. ______________________________
13. ______________________________
14. ______________________________
15. ______________________________
16. ______________________________
17. ______________________________
18. ______________________________
19. ______________________________
20. ______________________________

HOW I FEEL ABOUT MYSELF

AFFIRMATIONS: ANXIETY

1. In the big scheme of things, this isn't important.
2. Everything will work out in the way it was intended.
3. I do the best I can, and nobody can do more than that.
4. I am calm and relaxed.
5. I am prepared.
6. I am powerful & capable of great things, large and small.
7. I wrap myself in a world of peace.
8. I evaluate my problems & find solutions without emotion.
9. I am not worried.
10. I have control over my thoughts & the choices that I make.
11. ______________________________
12. ______________________________
13. ______________________________
14. ______________________________
15. ______________________________
16. ______________________________
17. ______________________________
18. ______________________________
19. ______________________________
20. ______________________________

HOW I FEEL ABOUT WORRYING

AFFIRMATIONS: PREJUDICE

1. I do not apologize for being myself.
2. I draw strength from those who have gone before me.
3. I treat others as equals and individuals.
4. I live in a world where I am judged for who I am.
5. I am a person, not a color.
6. People see me.
7. I forgive ignorance in others and help them learn.
8. I dare to be different and embrace my own uniqueness.
9. I see beyond the outward appearance of others.
10. People are more than an accident of birth.
11. ______________________________
12. ______________________________
13. ______________________________
14. ______________________________
15. ______________________________
16. ______________________________
17. ______________________________
18. ______________________________
19. ______________________________
20. ______________________________

HOW I FEEL ABOUT PREJUDICE

AFFIRMATIONS: CHARACTER

1. I am a natural leader.
2. I am strong and capable.
3. I am tenacious and never give up when things are difficult.
4. I am a hard worker.
5. I am kind and compassionate.
6. I am a well-rounded person with a variety of interests.
7. I am successful.
8. I am positive and look for the fun and humor in life.
9. I am loving and lovable.
10. I try to be the best "me" that I can me.
11. ______________________________
12. ______________________________
13. ______________________________
14. ______________________________
15. ______________________________
16. ______________________________
17. ______________________________
18. ______________________________
19. ______________________________
20. ______________________________

HOW I FEEL ABOUT MY CHARACTER

AFFIRMATIONS: SUCCESS

1. I believe in myself & my ability to do whatever I attempt.
2. I have what it takes.
3. I am not afraid of challenges and meet them head on.
4. I have faith in my dreams and ambitions.
5. I have the confidence to go after what I want.
6. I put my time and energy to good use.
7. I learn from my mistakes and use them to move forward.
8. I know my own worth.
9. They only person who can defeat me is myself.
10. I am brave enough to overcome any obstacles.
11. ______________________________
12. ______________________________
13. ______________________________
14. ______________________________
15. ______________________________
16. ______________________________
17. ______________________________
18. ______________________________
19. ______________________________
20. ______________________________

HOW I FEEL ABOUT SUCCESS

AFFIRMATIONS: HAPPINESS

1. I start each day with a positive attitude and a smile.
2. I take time to rest and to meditate.
3. I choose to be happy.
4. I have control over my feelings.
5. I'm in charge of how I want to feel today.
6. I conduct my life with enthusiasm and hope.
7. I am responsible for my own thoughts.
8. I accept the things that I cannot change.
9. I look for the silver lining in negative situations.
10. I am human & forgive myself for not being perfect.
11. ____________________
12. ____________________
13. ____________________
14. ____________________
15. ____________________
16. ____________________
17. ____________________
18. ____________________
19. ____________________
20. ____________________

HOW I FEEL ABOUT MY HAPPINESS

AFFIRMATIONS: THE FUTURE

1. I have the ability to change my story.
2. Life is what I choose to make it.
3. I am focused on achieving my goals.
4. My future is bright!
5. Wonderful things are going to happen to me.
6. I trust myself to create a better tomorrow.
7. I know where I've been and I know where I'm going.
8. I have achieved my goals.
9. I have a plan and move one step closer each day.
10. I look forward to the future and my role in it.
11. ______________________________
12. ______________________________
13. ______________________________
14. ______________________________
15. ______________________________
16. ______________________________
17. ______________________________
18. ______________________________
19. ______________________________
20. ______________________________

HOW I FEEL ABOUT MY FUTURE

MY MONTHLY AFFIRMATIONS

Choose your top affirmations to work on this month and repeat them to yourself at least once a day. Use the Affirmation Tracker to check them off!

1. ______________________________
2. ______________________________
3. ______________________________
4. ______________________________
5. ______________________________
6. ______________________________
7. ______________________________
8. ______________________________
9. ______________________________
10. ______________________________
11. ______________________________
12. ______________________________
13. ______________________________
14. ______________________________
15. ______________________________
16. ______________________________

AFFIRMATION TRACKER

Month ____________

Year ____________

Day	1	2	3	4	5	6	7	8	9	10	11	12	13	14	15	16
1																
2																
3																
4																
5																
6																
7																
8																
9																
10																
11																
12																
13																
14																
15																
16																
17																
18																
19																
20																
21																
22																
23																
24																
25																
26																
27																
28																
29																
30																
31																

MY MONTHLY AFFIRMATIONS

Choose your top affirmations to work on this month and repeat them to yourself at least once a day. Use the Affirmation Tracker to check them off!

1. ______________________________
2. ______________________________
3. ______________________________
4. ______________________________
5. ______________________________
6. ______________________________
7. ______________________________
8. ______________________________
9. ______________________________
10. ______________________________
11. ______________________________
12. ______________________________
13. ______________________________
14. ______________________________
15. ______________________________
16. ______________________________

AFFIRMATION TRACKER

Month ____________

Year ____________

Day	1	2	3	4	5	6	7	8	9	10	11	12	13	14	15	16
1																
2																
3																
4																
5																
6																
7																
8																
9																
10																
11																
12																
13																
14																
15																
16																
17																
18																
19																
20																
21																
22																
23																
24																
25																
26																
27																
28																
29																
30																
31																

MY MONTHLY AFFIRMATIONS

Choose your top affirmations to work on this month and repeat them to yourself at least once a day. Use the Affirmation Tracker to check them off!

1. ______________________________
2. ______________________________
3. ______________________________
4. ______________________________
5. ______________________________
6. ______________________________
7. ______________________________
8. ______________________________
9. ______________________________
10. ______________________________
11. ______________________________
12. ______________________________
13. ______________________________
14. ______________________________
15. ______________________________
16. ______________________________

AFFIRMATION TRACKER

Month ____________

Year ____________

Day	1	2	3	4	5	6	7	8	9	10	11	12	13	14	15	16
1																
2																
3																
4																
5																
6																
7																
8																
9																
10																
11																
12																
13																
14																
15																
16																
17																
18																
19																
20																
21																
22																
23																
24																
25																
26																
27																
28																
29																
30																
31																

MY MONTHLY AFFIRMATIONS

Choose your top affirmations to work on this month and repeat them to yourself at least once a day. Use the Affirmation Tracker to check them off!

1. ______________________________
2. ______________________________
3. ______________________________
4. ______________________________
5. ______________________________
6. ______________________________
7. ______________________________
8. ______________________________
9. ______________________________
10. ______________________________
11. ______________________________
12. ______________________________
13. ______________________________
14. ______________________________
15. ______________________________
16. ______________________________

AFFIRMATION TRACKER

Month ____________

Year ____________

Day	1	2	3	4	5	6	7	8	9	10	11	12	13	14	15	16
1																
2																
3																
4																
5																
6																
7																
8																
9																
10																
11																
12																
13																
14																
15																
16																
17																
18																
19																
20																
21																
22																
23																
24																
25																
26																
27																
28																
29																
30																
31																

MY MONTHLY AFFIRMATIONS

Choose your top affirmations to work on this month and repeat them to yourself at least once a day. Use the Affirmation Tracker to check them off!

1. ______________________________
2. ______________________________
3. ______________________________
4. ______________________________
5. ______________________________
6. ______________________________
7. ______________________________
8. ______________________________
9. ______________________________
10. ______________________________
11. ______________________________
12. ______________________________
13. ______________________________
14. ______________________________
15. ______________________________
16. ______________________________

AFFIRMATION TRACKER

Month ____________

Year ____________

Day	1	2	3	4	5	6	7	8	9	10	11	12	13	14	15	16
1																
2																
3																
4																
5																
6																
7																
8																
9																
10																
11																
12																
13																
14																
15																
16																
17																
18																
19																
20																
21																
22																
23																
24																
25																
26																
27																
28																
29																
30																
31																

MY MONTHLY AFFIRMATIONS

Choose your top affirmations to work on this month and repeat them to yourself at least once a day. Use the Affirmation Tracker to check them off!

1. ______________________________
2. ______________________________
3. ______________________________
4. ______________________________
5. ______________________________
6. ______________________________
7. ______________________________
8. ______________________________
9. ______________________________
10. ______________________________
11. ______________________________
12. ______________________________
13. ______________________________
14. ______________________________
15. ______________________________
16. ______________________________

AFFIRMATION TRACKER

Month ______________

Year ______________

Day	1	2	3	4	5	6	7	8	9	10	11	12	13	14	15	16
1																
2																
3																
4																
5																
6																
7																
8																
9																
10																
11																
12																
13																
14																
15																
16																
17																
18																
19																
20																
21																
22																
23																
24																
25																
26																
27																
28																
29																
30																
31																

MY MONTHLY AFFIRMATIONS

Choose your top affirmations to work on this month and repeat them to yourself at least once a day. Use the Affirmation Tracker to check them off!

1. ______________________________
2. ______________________________
3. ______________________________
4. ______________________________
5. ______________________________
6. ______________________________
7. ______________________________
8. ______________________________
9. ______________________________
10. ______________________________
11. ______________________________
12. ______________________________
13. ______________________________
14. ______________________________
15. ______________________________
16. ______________________________

AFFIRMATION TRACKER

Month ____________

Year ____________

Day	1	2	3	4	5	6	7	8	9	10	11	12	13	14	15	16
1																
2																
3																
4																
5																
6																
7																
8																
9																
10																
11																
12																
13																
14																
15																
16																
17																
18																
19																
20																
21																
22																
23																
24																
25																
26																
27																
28																
29																
30																
31																

MY MONTHLY AFFIRMATIONS

Choose your top affirmations to work on this month and repeat them to yourself at least once a day. Use the Affirmation Tracker to check them off!

1. ____________________
2. ____________________
3. ____________________
4. ____________________
5. ____________________
6. ____________________
7. ____________________
8. ____________________
9. ____________________
10. ____________________
11. ____________________
12. ____________________
13. ____________________
14. ____________________
15. ____________________
16. ____________________

AFFIRMATION TRACKER

Month ______________

Year ______________

Day	1	2	3	4	5	6	7	8	9	10	11	12	13	14	15	16
1																
2																
3																
4																
5																
6																
7																
8																
9																
10																
11																
12																
13																
14																
15																
16																
17																
18																
19																
20																
21																
22																
23																
24																
25																
26																
27																
28																
29																
30																
31																

MY MONTHLY AFFIRMATIONS

Choose your top affirmations to work on this month and repeat them to yourself at least once a day. Use the Affirmation Tracker to check them off!

1. ______________________________
2. ______________________________
3. ______________________________
4. ______________________________
5. ______________________________
6. ______________________________
7. ______________________________
8. ______________________________
9. ______________________________
10. ______________________________
11. ______________________________
12. ______________________________
13. ______________________________
14. ______________________________
15. ______________________________
16. ______________________________

AFFIRMATION TRACKER

Month ____________

Year ____________

Day	1	2	3	4	5	6	7	8	9	10	11	12	13	14	15	16
1																
2																
3																
4																
5																
6																
7																
8																
9																
10																
11																
12																
13																
14																
15																
16																
17																
18																
19																
20																
21																
22																
23																
24																
25																
26																
27																
28																
29																
30																
31																

MY MONTHLY AFFIRMATIONS

Choose your top affirmations to work on this month and repeat them to yourself at least once a day. Use the Affirmation Tracker to check them off!

1. ______________________________
2. ______________________________
3. ______________________________
4. ______________________________
5. ______________________________
6. ______________________________
7. ______________________________
8. ______________________________
9. ______________________________
10. ______________________________
11. ______________________________
12. ______________________________
13. ______________________________
14. ______________________________
15. ______________________________
16. ______________________________

AFFIRMATION TRACKER

Month ____________

Year ____________

Day	1	2	3	4	5	6	7	8	9	10	11	12	13	14	15	16
1																
2																
3																
4																
5																
6																
7																
8																
9																
10																
11																
12																
13																
14																
15																
16																
17																
18																
19																
20																
21																
22																
23																
24																
25																
26																
27																
28																
29																
30																
31																

MY MONTHLY AFFIRMATIONS

Choose your top affirmations to work on this month and repeat them to yourself at least once a day. Use the Affirmation Tracker to check them off!

1. ______________________________
2. ______________________________
3. ______________________________
4. ______________________________
5. ______________________________
6. ______________________________
7. ______________________________
8. ______________________________
9. ______________________________
10. ______________________________
11. ______________________________
12. ______________________________
13. ______________________________
14. ______________________________
15. ______________________________
16. ______________________________

AFFIRMATION TRACKER

Month ____________

Year ____________

Day	1	2	3	4	5	6	7	8	9	10	11	12	13	14	15	16
1																
2																
3																
4																
5																
6																
7																
8																
9																
10																
11																
12																
13																
14																
15																
16																
17																
18																
19																
20																
21																
22																
23																
24																
25																
26																
27																
28																
29																
30																
31																

MY MONTHLY AFFIRMATIONS

Choose your top affirmations to work on this month and repeat them to yourself at least once a day. Use the Affirmation Tracker to check them off!

1. ______________________________
2. ______________________________
3. ______________________________
4. ______________________________
5. ______________________________
6. ______________________________
7. ______________________________
8. ______________________________
9. ______________________________
10. ______________________________
11. ______________________________
12. ______________________________
13. ______________________________
14. ______________________________
15. ______________________________
16. ______________________________

AFFIRMATION TRACKER

Month ____________

Year ____________

Day	1	2	3	4	5	6	7	8	9	10	11	12	13	14	15	16
1																
2																
3																
4																
5																
6																
7																
8																
9																
10																
11																
12																
13																
14																
15																
16																
17																
18																
19																
20																
21																
22																
23																
24																
25																
26																
27																
28																
29																
30																
31																

NOTES

NOTES

NOTES

NOTES

NOTES

NOTES

NOTES

NOTES

NOTES

NOTES

NOTES

NOTES

NOTES

NOTES

NOTES

NOTES

NOTES

NOTES

NOTES

NOTES

NOTES

NOTES

NOTES

NOTES

Printed in Germany
by Amazon Distribution
GmbH, Leipzig

21161953R00043